Savitri's Tale
and Other
Heroic Stories

Written by Anthony Horowitz
Adapted by Trevor Baxendale
Illustrated by Simone Massoni

Published by Pearson Education Limited, Edinburgh Gate, Harlow, Essex, CM20 2JE

Registered company number: 872828

www.pearsonschools.co.uk

Adapted texts based on 'The Wishes of Savitri' from *Legends: Death and the Underworld*, first published by Macmillan Children's Books 2011; 'The Gorgon's Head' from *Legends: Beasts and Monsters*, first published by Macmillan Children's Books 2010; 'The Achilles Heel' from *Legends: Heroes and Villains*, first published by Macmillan Children's Books 2011

Copyright © Anthony Horowitz 2010, 2011

Adaptations by Trevor Baxendale

Authorised adaptations © Pearson Education Limited 2012

The right of Anthony Horowitz to be identified as author of the original works has been asserted by him in accordance with the Copyright, Designs and Patents Act 1988.

First published 2012

20

10 9 8 7

British Library Cataloguing in Publication Data

A catalogue record for this book is available from the British Library

ISBN 978 0 435 07576 7

Printed and bound in China by Golden Cup

Acknowledgements

We would like to thank the children and teachers of Bangor Central Integrated Primary School, NI; Bishop Henderson C of E Primary School, Somerset; Brookside Community Primary School, Somerset; Cheddington Combined School, Buckinghamshire; Cofton Primary School, Birmingham; Dair House Independent School, Buckinghamshire; Deal Parochial School, Kent; Holy Trinity Catholic Primary School, Chipping Norton; Lawthorn Primry School, North Ayrshire; Newbold Riverside Primary School, Rugby and Windmill Primary School, Oxford for their invaluable help in the development and trialling of the Bug Club resources.

Every effort has been made to contact copyright holders of material reproduced in this book. Any omissions will be rectified in subsequent printings if notice is given to the publisher.

Contents

Scamblesby C E Primary
School
Scamblesby
Louth
Lincs
LN11 9XG

Tel No: 01507 343629

Savitri's Tale

INDIA

Savitri

Satyavan

Yama, god of death

Savitri was an Indian princess who preferred to read and study the scriptures, rather than dance and spend time with potential suitors. This concerned her father, the king, who wanted her to take a husband. When she was eighteen, Savitri's father suggested that she should marry, as was the custom, but the princess gently declined.

"My dear father," she said, "I am not yet ready to marry. First let me travel for a year, praying at the shrines and listening to the words of the holy men."

"But Savitri," the king replied, "you are already eighteen. You should marry."

"If I am to be married, destiny will find me a husband," the princess laughingly replied.

So Savitri wandered for a year, meeting holy men up and down the country. She ate the simplest food and slept under the stars. To meet her, none would have guessed that she was a princess.

Eventually her travels brought her to a forest where she struck up a conversation with a tall, handsome man. He was carrying an axe in one hand and a bundle of firewood in the other.

"My name is Satyavan," the young man said. "My father was born a king, but in his old age he lost his sight and then his kingdom. Now we live in poverty, in a small cottage in the forest. It is a difficult life for my poor father. I take him wood for fuel, but I wish that I could provide something that would comfort him more!"

When Savitri returned to her own palace, she announced that she intended to marry Satyavan. Narada, a holy man who knew everything that there was to know, was dismayed.

"You must not marry this man, Savitri,"
he said.

"Why ever not?" Savitri asked.

"Because he is living under a curse. One
year from now you will be not a wife but a
widow."

However, Savitri had already promised
herself to Satyavan and the wedding took
place. Savitri put away all her jewels and
fine clothes and went to live in the forest as
Satyavan's devoted wife.

Never once did she tell her husband what Narada had foreseen, but never for a minute could she forget it. If Satyavan had an appointment with the god of death, then nothing could come between the two of them. For it is often said in India that Yama, the god of death, is the only god who never breaks his word.

Sure enough, after twelve months, Yama paid them a visit.

One beautiful summer's day, Satyavan was working while Savitri sang to him. Suddenly, he dropped his axe and stumbled. Cold with dread, Savitri caught him just as he fell.

The glade was immediately thrown into shadow. When Savitri looked up, she saw a figure dressed in black, a noose of rough rope clasped in one hand. Savitri knew at once that this was Yama.

"Savitri," he said, "I claim the soul of Satyavan as is my right. Do not be afraid for him. All his sorrows are now over."

Yama leaned down and fastened the rope around the dying man's head. At the touch of the rope, the soul of Satyavan separated from his body, and stood up to follow Yama.

"Farewell," Yama said. "And remember – I am the only god to whom everyone is faithful. One day you and I will meet again."

He turned and walked away but, driven by an instinct that made her forget her fear, Savitri followed. Hearing her, Yama turned again and now two black flames flickered where his eyes should have been, for his head had become a skull and his body, beneath the robes, a bare skeleton. Savitri was unafraid.

"I see that you have more courage than sense," said Yama, "for who would willingly follow the god of death? Very well – I will bequeath you a gift to help soothe your grief. You may ask for anything you like except for the life of your husband."

"Then I ask for my father-in-law's sight to be returned," Savitri said.

"It is granted," Yama said. "Now farewell again."

For a second time, the god of death departed, leading the soul of Satyavan behind him. Now the forest grew wild. Thistles sprang up and thorns pressed in on the path, but still Savitri followed.

"I shall grant you a further wish," Yama said, angrily, "but once again you may not ask for your husband's life!"

"Then I would like my father-in-law's kingdom and his wealth to be returned to him," Savitri said.

"It is done. Now leave me!"

Savitri continued to follow Yama. The forest grew ever darker and more savage.

"Still here!"
exclaimed Yama in
all his fury when
he turned round
for a third time.
"Never has a
mortal so defied
me! Very well.
One last wish
will I grant you
but then you and I
must part company,
or I shall take you to
my shadowy kingdom
too. So far you have favoured
only your father-in-law. What can I bestow
upon you for yourself?"

"Only this," Savitri said. "Grant that I
may have many children and that I should
live to see their children's children grow up
in health and happiness. Will you give me
this, great Yama?"

"It is a good wish," Yama said with a smile, "and I grant it."

Then it was Savitri's turn to smile. "You have forgotten," she said, "that according to Hindu law, a widow does not remarry."

Yama thought for a moment, realising how he had been tricked. If Savitri could not remarry, then how could she have children and grandchildren? And yet that was what he had promised her, he who never broke his word. In which case …

For a second, Savitri thought the god of death was going to strike her down where she stood, but then the forest rang with the sound of his laughter and he removed the noose from Satyavan's neck.

"It is a courageous woman who would follow her husband into the grave," he said, "and who would also trick the god of death himself. Very well, Savitri. I will give you back the only man who can be the father of your children. It will be a long, long time before the two of us meet again. Go in peace, for your devotion to Satyavan has defeated me."

Savitri and Satyavan returned home to discover that the sight and the fortunes of the old king had indeed been restored. Thus began a long and happy life in which they were forever true to one another, in life and, eventually, in death.

The Gorgon's Head

GREECE

AEGEAN SEA

Seriphos

Perseus

Polydectes

Medusa

Athene, Goddess of Wisdom

There was once a king called Polydectes who ruled over an island called Seriphos. Like many rulers in Ancient Greece, he was cruel and thoughtless and took what he wanted without considering anyone else.

Now Polydectes had fallen in love with a beautiful woman called Danaë and was determined to make her his wife. Unfortunately, Danaë didn't quite have the same feelings about Polydectes. This was hardly surprising. The king was overweight, with bad breath and a foul temper.

Left to himself, Polydectes would have forced Danaë to marry him, but there was her son to consider. Perseus was strong, fearless and quick-tempered … in short, just the sort to let fly with a sword if anyone laid a finger on his mother. He was also extremely popular and there would have been uproar had he met with an unfortunate 'accident'.

However, the king had a plan. He announced his marriage, but pretended that he was going to marry someone else.

As was the custom, everybody gave expensive gifts to show how loyal they were to the king. Everyone, that is, with one exception.

Poor Perseus was just a soldier, and couldn't possibly afford a lavish present. Of course, Polydectes knew this. It was all part of his plan.

"What, no wedding present?" he shouted, when Perseus arrived at the wedding feast.

There were gasps of surprise around the banqueting tables.

"I'm very sorry, Your Majesty …" Perseus began.

"Surely you know that it is a tradition to bring your king a present when he decides to get married?"

"I'm afraid I cannot afford a suitable gift."

"That's no excuse. Coming here empty-handed is an outrage. It's nothing short of treason!"

"I didn't intend to insult you, sire. You can have anything you want for your wedding present. You only have to name it."

"Anything?" Polydectes asked, raising an eyebrow.

"Anything in the world," promised Perseus rashly. He really didn't want to upset the king, and the king knew it.

"All right," the king said. "If you really want to prove your loyalty to me, bring me the head of the Gorgon."

There was a stunned silence in the room. Nobody moved.

"Very well, Your Majesty," Perseus said. "If the head of the Gorgon is what you desire, the head of the Gorgon is what you shall have."

With that, Perseus turned on his heel and left. The king waited until he was sure Perseus had departed, and then seized his mother. "I insist that you come to my wedding," he announced.

"It will be my pleasure, Your Majesty," Danaë muttered.

"Of course it will be your pleasure, darling. You're the one I'm marrying!"

Of all the beasts, giants, dragons and demigods in Ancient Greece, the Gorgon was the most terrifying. Her name was Medusa. Instead of teeth she had sharp tusks. Her hands were made of bronze, and golden wings sprouted from her shoulders. But what was most remarkable about the Gorgon was her hair. It was made of dozens of living snakes, green and silver with hissing tongues, writhing over her forehead and curling around her shoulders.

The Gorgon petrified people – quite literally.

For this was the cruellest part of the trick that King Polydectes had played on the unwitting Perseus. Anyone who saw the face of the Gorgon became so frightened that they instantly turned to stone. Polydectes knew that Perseus would never get anywhere near Medusa: just one glance in her direction and he would be doomed.

Perseus searched far and wide but he found no trace of Medusa. Indeed, most of the travellers he encountered seemed unwilling to talk about her at all.

One night he found himself sitting under a tree on the edge of a swamp. He was in an unknown country, feeling cold, alone and seriously regretting ever agreeing to the king's request.

It was at that moment that a figure suddenly appeared, stepping out of the flames of the bonfire he had built to warm himself.

It was a woman, tall and imperious, with bright, purposeful eyes. Perseus recognised her at once as Athene, the Goddess of Wisdom.

"Perseus," she said, standing in front of him, "I've come to help you. You have a good heart and I know that one day you will be a great hero, but you are also young and foolish and you have allowed King Polydectes to trick you."

"Thank you, great Athene," Perseus said. "I do need your help ..."

"I know who you're looking for and I've decided to assist you in your quest. Firstly, the only way to find the Gorgon is to ask her sisters – the Grey Ones."

"Where will I find them?" Perseus asked.

"They live in the swamp, a few minutes' walk from here. But listen to me, Perseus. You will have to be very careful about how you kill Medusa. Whoever sets eyes on her turns to stone."

"You mean ... I can't even glance at her?"

"Not directly, no." Athene laughed briefly and coldly. "Polydectes didn't tell you that little detail, did he? Never mind, I can show you what to do. Just listen carefully to my instructions, Perseus. Your life will depend on it ..."

A short while later, Perseus crept up on the Grey Ones, who were sitting beside a stinking bog. They were arguing, as always.

The Grey Ones weren't exactly monsters but they were certainly very strange. They had only one eye and one tooth between the three of them. Their names were Enyo, Pemphredo and Deino and as Perseus approached, this is what he overheard.

"Can I have
the tooth please,
Enyo?" Pemphredo
was saying.

"Why?" Enyo asked.

"Because I want to eat an apple."

"I'm chewing a toffee just now."

"You can suck the
toffee. I need the
tooth!"

"All right, all right.
Here it is, then."

"I can't see it."

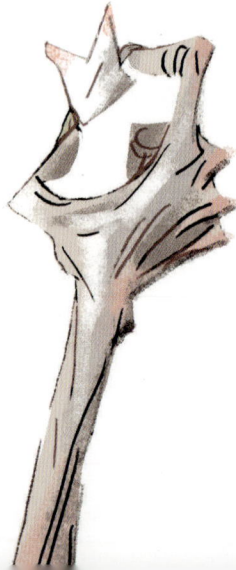

"Haven't you got the eye?"

"I've got the eye," Deino said.

"Let me have it," Pemphredo demanded.

"No. I'm looking at something."

The argument carried on and on and Perseus guessed that the three old hags must have had the same conversation day in, day out. Silently, he tiptoed up behind them and snatched away both the eye and the tooth, saying, "I have your eye and your tooth and I won't return them until you tell me where I can find your sister, Medusa."

The three Grey Ones got up and tried to grab him, but being unable to see, they only grabbed each other. Eventually they sat down again, banging their fists in the mud with frustration.

"If you don't give me the information I need," Perseus continued, "I'll throw your eye and your tooth away and you'll never see anyone or bite anything again."

"Go to the Land of the Hyperboreans," Enyo said. Her voice was shrill and bitter. "There's a cavern in a valley there. You can't miss it."

"That's where you'll find our sister," Pemphredo added. "Just make sure you take a good look at her."

"Look her straight in the eyes!" Deino giggled. "You'll never forget your first sight of Medusa."

Perseus returned the eye and the tooth and set off, the Grey Ones' laughter echoing in his ears.

Athene had not only advised Perseus
how to destroy the Gorgon, she had given
him the means. As he approached Medusa's
lair, he carried the goddess' brightly
polished shield in one hand and his own
sword in the other. At last, he found
himself in a narrow cavern, surrounded
by statues of men, women and children;
all had been frozen in horror at the sight
of the Gorgon.

A shudder washed over Perseus and

he took a deep breath as he crept into Medusa's cave.

"Medusa!" he called out. His voice sounded lost in the shadows.

Something moved at the back of the cave.

"Medusa!" Perseus repeated.

Now he could hear the sound of hissing.

"I am Perseus!" he announced.

"Perseus!" came a deep, throaty voice from the back of the cave. "Have you come to see me?"

The Gorgon stepped forward into the light. For a dreadful moment, Perseus was tempted to look up at her, to meet her eyes but, using all his willpower, he kept his head turned away just as Athene had instructed him. Instead, he concentrated on the reflection in his shield. He could see the Gorgon's green skin, yellow tusks and poisonous red eyes reflected in the polished bronze.

"Look at me! Look at me!" the Gorgon cried.

Still Perseus kept his eyes on the shield as he stepped further into the cave. The

Gorgon's reflection was huge, the tusks snarling at him out of the shield, the snakes writhing furiously.

"Look at me! Look at me!"

"No!"

With a despairing cry, Perseus swung wildly with his sword. He felt the sharp steel bite into flesh and bone. The Gorgon screamed. The snakes hissed as her head flew from her shoulders. A fountain of blood spouted out of Medusa's neck as her body crumpled. When at last it was over, and with his eyes still fixed on the shield, Perseus picked up the grim trophy of his victory and dropped it into a sack.

Perseus had spent months seeking the Gorgon and took part in many adventures on his way home. By the time he arrived back on Seriphos, a whole year had passed.

The first person he saw on the island was an old friend, a fisherman who was just bringing in the morning catch.

"Tell me," Perseus said, "has the king married?"

"No," the fisherman said. "King Polydectes lives alone."

"And how fares my mother?" Perseus asked.

At this, the fisherman burst into tears. "Oh Master Perseus!" he cried. "It was your mother whom the wicked king wished to marry. When she refused him, he enslaved her ..."

"We'll soon see about that!" Perseus said through gritted teeth. Throwing the sack that he carried over his shoulder, Perseus strode into the palace and straight into the great hall where King Polydectes was sitting on his throne.

"Greetings, Your Majesty!" Perseus called out to the astonished monarch. "It is I, Perseus. I bring with me the gift that you requested."

"The Gorgon's head?" Polydectes muttered. He pointed at the sack. "Have you got it there?"

"See for yourself." Perseus lifted the Gorgon's head out of the sack and held it up for the king to inspect.

"It's …" King Polydectes got no further than that. What was he about to say? It's hideous? It's not possible? Nobody would ever know. Instantly, a stone statue leaned out from the throne, a stone sneer on its stone face.

No sooner had Polydectes been petrified than a great cheer began to travel around the throne room and spread throughout the palace. Everyone on the island detested their cruel and scheming monarch.

Perseus was reunited with his mother and, after many more adventures, he became King of Mycenae. Athene's prophecy had been correct – Perseus had a good heart and was born to be a hero.

As for Polydectes, he was put in the palace garden as an ornament, and he is probably still there to this day.

Achilles' Heel

GREECE

AEGEAN SEA

Troy

Achilles

Patroclus

Hector

This is the story of the greatest of all the Greek heroes: Achilles. Achilles the fierce; the strong; the most courageous man who ever lived.

Achilles' mother, Thetis, was immortal but his father, the King of the Myrmidons, was mortal. Thetis could not bear the thought of her only son growing old and weak while she lived forever. So when Achilles was born, Thetis took him away and, holding him by one heel, dipped her child in the magical River Styx to make him immortal too. However, she made a mistake that was one day to prove fatal – she forgot to immerse the heel itself and that part of Achilles remained mortal.

Achilles grew into a strong, handsome youth. His body was broad-shouldered and muscular and his hair was a mass of golden curls. Legend has it that at the age of six he could outrun a full-grown stag and kill it with his own hands.

But while Achilles was growing up, the clouds of war were gathering.

Menelaus,
King of
Sparta and leader
of the Greek forces,
was preparing for war
with the city of Troy. A
Trojan called Paris had stolen his
beautiful wife Helen, and Menelaus
wanted her back. With Menelaus was his
brother, Agamemnon, King of Mycenae, and
Odysseus, King of Ithaca. Odysseus sought
to recruit Achilles into their army because a
soothsayer had warned him that Troy could
not be taken without his help. Achilles was
accompanied by his cousin, Patroclus, whom
Achilles loved more than anyone else in the
world. Patroclus was older than Achilles but
less skilful in combat …

Their first battle was fought on the beach near Troy, and Achilles, leading his father's faithful Myrmidons, quickly proved that he deserved his reputation for valour. In the first twenty minutes of the battle he had killed no fewer than a hundred Trojans, and his armour dripped red with their blood.

In the weeks that followed, Achilles added victory to victory, until his name was the most feared of all within the entire Greek army. Priam, the King of Troy, lost no fewer than three of his sons at the hand of Achilles. Priam's beloved son Troilus was even chased into the Temple of Apollo and speared on the very altar itself.

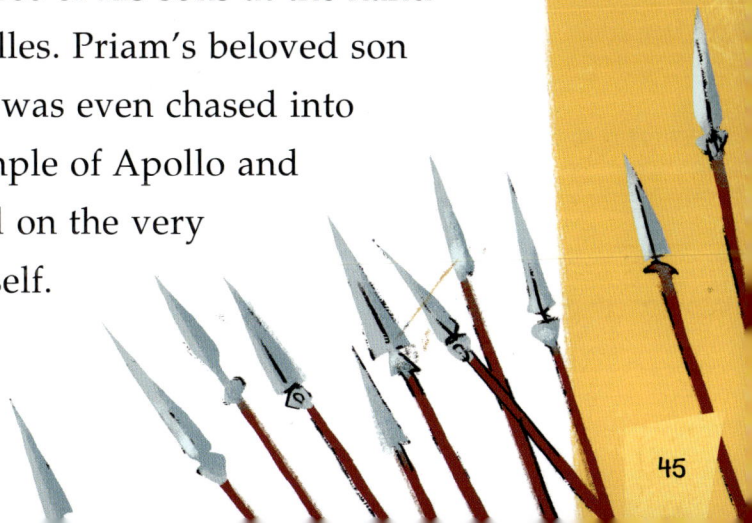

It was during this time that Achilles had an argument with Agamemnon over a woman. Achilles was so furious, he retired to his tent and refused to have anything more to do with the war.

At first, nobody believed that so great a warrior could behave in such a way, but as the days passed, they realised that Achilles was serious about withdrawing from battle. The Trojans, when their spies reported the news, returned to the battlefield with renewed vigour. After all, this was virtually

their first piece of good fortune since the Greeks had landed.

Suddenly it seemed that the Trojans had gained the upper hand. A daring attack was led by Hector, the eldest son of King Priam, and the Greek defences were broken. Both Agamemnon and Odysseus were wounded in the fighting and while the Greeks scattered in panic, Hector seized the opportunity to advance on their fleet.

Fortunately, Patroclus, the cousin of
Achilles, saved the day. Wearing the armour
of Achilles, he stormed through the clouds
of black smoke rising from the ships and
hurled his spear into the mass of Trojans.
His resemblance to Achilles was so strong
that the Trojans mistook him for his cousin
and fled.

Now Patroclus had lived
his whole life in the shadow
of Achilles. Where his cousin
had been glorified, he had been
ignored. Suddenly, he found
himself a hero in his own right.
He pursued the Trojans right
back to the city walls, while
Achilles, hearing what was
happening, hastily assembled
his Myrmidons. At this point,
Patroclus' luck ran out. A chance
blow caught him between the
shoulder-blades and a sword was
driven into his chest. Dying, he
tried to lift himself out of the
mud. That was how Hector found
him. One blow and it was over.

When Achilles found the body of his cousin, the Greek soldiers were fighting furiously to protect it. With a cry of anger and grief, Achilles threw himself into the battle, striking out left and right, forming a bloody circle around the corpse. Eventually, as the sun was setting, the Trojans retreated and Achilles salvaged the body of Patroclus.

He was buried beside the sea, the dying sun casting a scarlet banner across the water. Agamemnon, though wounded, came from his tent to make his peace with Achilles, and Achilles, standing beside his cousin's grave, swore revenge on Hector, the man who had killed him.

If Achilles was the pride of the Greek army, then Hector was his equivalent among the Trojans. The men were natural opponents and although the two had yet to meet in battle, each sought revenge on the other – Achilles for the death of Patroclus, Hector for the loss of three brothers.

Hector had previously challenged Achilles to single combat during the time when Achilles was refusing to fight. Now he had good reason to take Hector on, and for one day the war was suspended; both sides stood back to watch the confrontation.

It was a bright morning. The gates of Troy swung open and Hector stepped forward, dressed in black and silver armour, a sword in one hand, a spear in the other. Then the flaps of Achilles' tent were pulled back and the murmur became a gasp. Achilles emerged, wearing dazzling armour that seemed to be carved out of solid gold. The reflection of the sun around him was blinding and perhaps Hector knew at that moment that he was doomed.

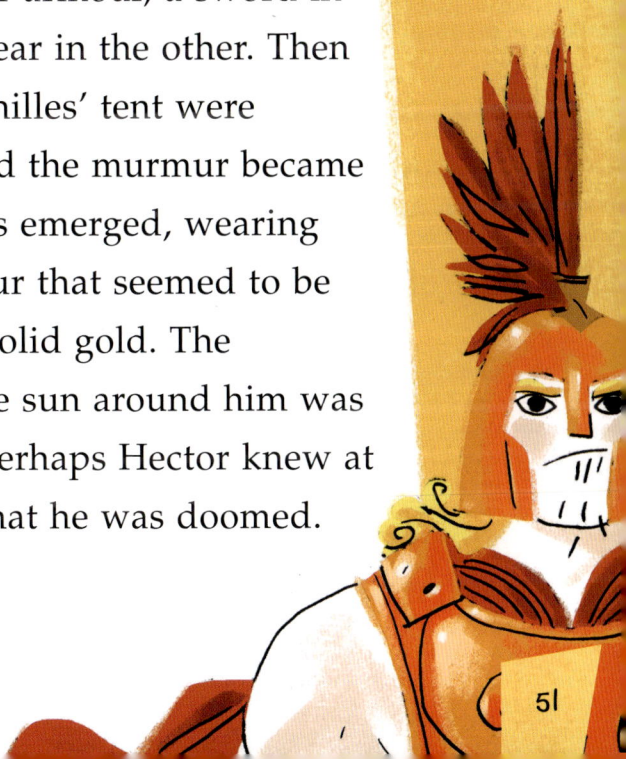

Achilles was relentless, unstoppable. Without speaking, he approached the Trojan, his feet pounding in the dust. As soon as he was within range, Hector hurled his spear. Achilles raised his shield and the spear clattered uselessly to one side. Then Hector took flight; not because he was afraid but because he hoped to tire his enemy. Three times he circled the walls of Troy but when he paused and looked round, Achilles was still the same distance from him, barely out of breath.

Finally, with the shouts of the Trojan forces above them and the Greek forces all around them, the two men joined in combat. So ferociously did they fight that when sword struck sword the spark could be seen a mile away. Hector was stronger but Achilles was faster and, watching from the walls, the Trojans let out a great cry when he dodged a blow, carried his sword in low and ran Hector through the heart.

Hector crumpled to his knees.

"Achilles!" he whispered. "Let my parents have my body. Let me be buried honourably."

"Never!" Achilles cried, still grieving for Patroclus and desperate to avenge his death. He twisted his sword and watched the light in Hector's eyes go out.

Achilles took Hector's body and, while King Priam looked on, helpless and in horror, he fastened it by the feet to his chariot and rode off around the city. Three more times he circled Troy, dragging its dead hero behind him.

At last, the gates of Troy opened and King Priam himself rode out. Under the flag of truce, he proceeded to the tent of Achilles and there threw himself on to the ground.

"Achilles!" the old man wept. "You have proved yourself a great warrior, but have you the compassion to prove yourself a great man? You have killed the son I most loved and in whom I had most pride. Now, I beg you, show pity to an old man. See – I bring you Hector's weight in gold. Will you not be moved by a father's tears? Let me bury my son."

Then Achilles wept too – for his cousin Patroclus, for the futility of war and for the sort of man he had almost become himself. He gave orders for the body of Hector to be carried back to Troy and called for a truce of twelve days in which the funeral could be prepared.

The war dragged on, and for Achilles, time was running out. After the death of

Hector, he fought as bravely as ever, but he had made himself the target of too many enemies, and not all of them were human.

The god Apollo had been enraged by the killing of Troilus, which had taken place in Apollo's own temple. Apollo recalled how Thetis had held Achilles when she dipped him in the River Styx. One day, in the thick of battle, Paris – the man who had begun the war by stealing Helen away – let loose a poisoned arrow which Apollo diverted to strike Achilles' heel.

At once, Achilles fainted and was carried off the battlefield by his Myrmidons. Doctors were called but the poison was already coursing through his blood. That night, with Thetis beside him and the stars blazing silver in the sky, Achilles died.

The Greek army mourned for seventeen days and seventeen nights. On the eighteenth day, Achilles' body was burned on a great pyre beside the sea.

And as the smoke rose over the crashing waves, the two armies clashed once again in a war which was now tainted by grey despair, a war which was suddenly less glorious and less heroic than it had once seemed.